GW00420438

TIPPING THE SCALES PRESS

Published by *Tipping the Scales* publishing press
and *Tipping the Scales Literary & Arts Journal*,
Suffolk, UK.

www.tippingthescalesjo.wixsite.com/mysite
First published in January 2021

Welcome!

Maybe you found this book because you get stuck in the same patterns. Perhaps you did a few Google searches and came up with writing prompts that were a bit disappointing. (Imagine you are an alien, what would you eat for dinner? Not that inspiring). Maybe the pandemic has you feeling stuck creatively.

We decided to write these prompts to inspire you to dig a bit deeper than the typical internet search prompts to get you out of that slump and into writing literature, poetry, creative non-fiction or just writing for the fun of it.

Some prompts may not inspire you, skip them. Others may help you to start a longer piece. The goal is to get yourself into the habit of writing, even if you don't feel like you can think of anything to write.

We all have a nice fairy and a critical fairy. One on each shoulder. Let the nice one help you write your first draft. Then bring out the critical fairy and let her fix the errors. If you bring out the critical fairy first, your writing will not be as carefree or honest. You will be spending too much time trying to be perfect. (Not that we have any experience with that or anything) Try to allow your writing to just flow out of you and enjoy the process.

Suggested ways to use this journal:

Visit **our Pinterest page** (The page is called "Not the Writing Prompts You Find on the Internet") that we made for this book to visually inspire you.

Daily inspirations to aid the creative process.

Choose a theme or book that you are planning to write and use these prompts as ideas or inspiration for scenes in your story.

Write every day, or use this when you need inspiration.

Start an online writer's group and inspire your friends to write with you.

Practice and explore different genres, themes and writing techniques as well as creating and staying in character, and writing believable dialogue.

We wish you the best in all of your writing endeavours!

Lori and Natascha Graham

1. Write a short flash fiction piece, then re-write the piece three times in the styles of Virginia Woolf, Douglas Adams and Julia Donaldson to see how the different writing styles alter the story, characters and feeling.

_____

_____

_____

_____

_____

_____

_____

_____

_____

_____

_____

2. Write the POV of a historical figure or writer that you admire (Or hate).

_____

_____

_____

_____

_____

_____

_____

_____

_____

_____

_____

_____

_____

3. Find a famous (or not famous) poem that you like. Rewrite the poem in your own words, trying to keep the main structure. If it is a positive poem, make it negative. If it is a sad or angry poem, make it more uplifting.

_____

_____

_____

_____

_____

_____

_____

_____

_____

_____

_____

_____

_____

4. Write the fictional retelling of a real moment in history.

_____

_____

_____

_____

_____

_____

_____

_____

_____

_____

_____

_____

_____

5. Describe a dove on a telephone wire on a winter morning.

_____

_____

_____

_____

_____

_____

_____

_____

_____

_____

_____

_____

_____

6. Write down the recipe for your favourite childhood food and a memory of eating it or how it made you feel while eating it.

_____

_____

_____

_____

_____

_____

_____

_____

_____

_____

_____

_____

_____

7. Write about a garden that you would love to have. What kinds of flowers would you grow? Would it be small? Or would it have all flowers and tall trees like the Secret Garden? Would you have vegetables? Would you plant all colours mixed up? Would you have sections of sections of purple, etc… Would your garden have a fountain? A table to sit and admire nature? Would you like to be alone? What kinds of birds visit? Once you have finished describing your ideal garden, try to take the words that you used and write a poem.

_____

_____

_____

_____

_____

_____

_____

_____

_____

_____

8. Writing in the first person, imagine you are one of the following, and write a fragment of your life:
A young girl travelling with her family in a covered wagon going west across America in 1897.
A young girl living alone in a stately home in 1900 England.
A young girl in poverty living in London, in 1837.

_____

_____

_____

_____

_____

_____

_____

_____

_____

_____

_____

_____

9. Use this picture to inspire you to write an ekphrastic poem (A poem that is inspired by a painting, photo or work of art, look at Pinterest for inspiration).

_____

_____

_____

_____

_____

_____

_____

_____

_____

_____

_____

_____

_____

10. Take two characters from two different books or TV shows and write about them meeting.

_____

_____

_____

_____

_____

_____

_____

_____

_____

_____

_____

_____

_____

11. Take a page from a newspaper or an old book that has plenty of words on it. Write a blackout poem by circling the words you want to use and blacking out the rest. This can be done with black marker, paint, or by making a painting around the words. Tape or glue that on this page (or we can make a page with words for the poem. (pinterest has some lovely examples for Blackout poetry)

_____

_____

_____

_____

_____

_____

_____

_____

_____

_____

_____

_____

12. Read or watch Julia Donaldson's The Gruffalo and invent an imaginary creature of your own. Write a short story about what they get up to and their adventures.

_____

_____

_____

_____

_____

_____

_____

_____

_____

_____

_____

_____

_____

13. Challenge yourself to write a short story that can be enjoyed by a reader of any age.

_____

_____

_____

_____

_____

_____

_____

_____

_____

_____

_____

_____

_____

14. Write a rhyming children's story that has a definite beginning, middle and end.

_____

_____

_____

_____

_____

_____

_____

_____

_____

_____

_____

_____

_____

15. Turn a dream into a story. If you don't dream, or can't remember any dreams, go to Google and type in "My dream last night" and find one that you can use for your writing.

_____

_____

_____

_____

_____

_____

_____

_____

_____

_____

_____

_____

16. Write the same characters day four times, one in each season and explore how the season's change the way in which the character feels, and how they go about their day.

_____

_____

_____

_____

_____

_____

_____

_____

_____

_____

_____

_____

_____

17. Go and visit a cemetery and write a story of someone with a name you find on a gravestone.

_____

_____

_____

_____

_____

_____

_____

_____

_____

_____

_____

_____

_____

18. Write the story of a woman who is named after a fruit. E.g, Clementine, Apple, etc. What sort of person are they and how does their unusual name interact with their life?

_____

_____

_____

_____

_____

_____

_____

_____

_____

_____

_____

_____

_____

19. Write the voices of three (or more) people from the same family having a conversation in the kitchen while lunch is being cooked.

_____

_____

_____

_____

_____

_____

_____

_____

_____

_____

_____

_____

_____

20. Tell the story of an imaginary collection of characters who live in a tree.

_____

_____

_____

_____

_____

_____

_____

_____

_____

_____

_____

_____

_____

_____

21. Imagine that a person in your past who has died comes to you in a unique or interesting way. Write a flash fiction story about that encounter. For example, whenever you spray perfume, your mother appears in the bathroom to have a chat.

_____

_____

_____

_____

_____

_____

_____

_____

_____

_____

_____

_____

22. Pick a book off your bookshelf. Go to pages 7, 20, and 21. Write down the fifth word in the second paragraph for each page. (You can leave out words like the, and, I, etc...) and use those three words to write a story or poem.

_____

_____

_____

_____

_____

_____

_____

_____

_____

_____

_____

_____

23. Take a walk outside and find a tree in your neighborhood or an area you walk often (If you live in the city and can't find a tree, use Pinterest to find a tree that speaks to you). Imagine that the tree has memories and feelings. Imagine a story told from the perspective of the tree.

_____

_____

_____

_____

_____

_____

_____

_____

_____

_____

_____

_____

24. Create a Pinterest board of images to inspire you and use one for a story or scene of a story.

_____

_____

_____

_____

_____

_____

_____

_____

_____

_____

_____

_____

25. Find a picture of a house you could imagine being haunted and write the story of the ghost or ghosts who live there ("Ghost House" brings up some amazing images).

_____

_____

_____

_____

_____

_____

_____

_____

_____

_____

_____

_____

26. Write the story of two women who swap books (or notes in books) in a book swap phone box but never meet.

_____

_____

_____

_____

_____

_____

_____

_____

_____

_____

_____

_____

_____

_____

27. Think of an author that you really admire. Someone you turn to often to read for inspiration. Find something that they wrote, read it several times, and try a story or poem in the style that they write.

_____

_____

_____

_____

_____

_____

_____

_____

_____

_____

_____

_____

_____

28. Walk around your house and take 10 words from either book titles, cereal boxes, fridge magnets, or anything that you see on a daily basis (without opening any books). Try to find words that you like, words that make you feel something, words that give you a tiny spark of an idea. Use those 10 words in a poem or story. If you are feeling very creative, use only those 10 words.

_____

_____

_____

_____

_____

_____

_____

_____

_____

_____

_____

31, Write about finding a lost item that seems to have some sort of energy or power.

_____

_____

_____

_____

_____

_____

_____

_____

_____

_____

_____

_____

_____

32. Investigate the life of a real life unknown female from the past (i.e. a woman in the land army) and tell her story.

_____

_____

_____

_____

_____

_____

_____

_____

_____

_____

_____

_____

_____

_____

33. Do some investigative journalism on something that you are interested in. As you gather information, write down key words that stand out to you. Take those words and try to arrange them in a poem or story. Make the writing personal to you and the subject that interests you.

_____

_____

_____

_____

_____

_____

_____

_____

_____

_____

_____

_____

34. Write the diary entry of a historical figure during a very mundane or typical day.

_____

_____

_____

_____

_____

_____

_____

_____

_____

_____

_____

_____

_____

_____

35. Write about a woman called Hyacinth who knows the language of flowers.

_____

_____

_____

_____

_____

_____

_____

_____

_____

_____

_____

_____

_____

_____

36. Research a random village in a country you've never been to (and preferably never heard of) and tell the story of someone from there.

_____

_____

_____

_____

_____

_____

_____

_____

_____

_____

_____

_____

_____

37. Visit our Pinterest board and use an image for writing inspiration

_____

_____

_____

_____

_____

_____

_____

_____

_____

_____

_____

_____

_____

38. Use Google or Pinterest (or any place you find pictures). type in the words "Magical forest." and choose a picture that you like. (If this is not something you are interested in, try a word that makes you happy. How about "Blue Lagoon," "Beaches at Night" or Northern Lights?) Find a quote or a picture that makes you stop when scrolling. Write your thoughts and feelings about why that picture spoke to you. Try to dig deep.

_____

_____

_____

_____

_____

_____

_____

_____

_____

_____

_____

_____

39. Come up with you-centred self-care ideas, like lists of little things that help you to feel better when you are feeling anxious, trapped, depressed, stuck or creatively hindered in some way.

_____

_____

_____

_____

_____

_____

_____

_____

_____

_____

_____

_____

_____

_____

40. Investigate a local folklore or myth and write something inspired by it.

_____

_____

_____

_____

_____

_____

_____

_____

_____

_____

_____

_____

_____

_____

41. Write a story for children that you wish you could have read when you were a young child.

_____

_____

_____

_____

_____

_____

_____

_____

_____

_____

_____

_____

_____

_____

42. What is a memory that you have of a grandparent? Is there something that makes you think of them (whether or not they are still around). Is there a smell that reminds you of them? A type of food? Is there a sound that makes you remember something about them? Think of a specific memory and try to describe the way it looked, sounded, smelled, were you eating or drinking anything special, what did the food taste like, how did you feel? Give as much detail as possible. Is there a fabric, perfume, item of clothing, or place that you think of when you think about that grandparent? (If you don't want to write about a grandparent, use a parent, partner, friend, child, etc.)

_____

_____

_____

_____

_____

_____

_____

_____

_____

_____

43. Write a story of a woman who is self-sufficient and completely isolated. She has to grow everything she eats and only has the company of nature.

_____

_____

_____

_____

_____

_____

_____

_____

_____

_____

_____

_____

_____

44. Write a story of a little girl who visits her
grandmother's old mansion and everytime she goes there
she plays with the buttons in an old button tin and goes
on adventures with the ghosts/people whose clothes the
buttons came from.

_____

_____

_____

_____

_____

_____

_____

_____

_____

_____

_____

_____

45. Tell the story of an animal (bird, bug, slug, snail, bunny etc) that you see in your garden. Give it a name and a life story.

_____

_____

_____

_____

_____

_____

_____

_____

_____

_____

_____

_____

_____

_____

46. Write the story of a woman who leaves gifts she has made on the doorsteps of everyone in her village. Who is she, why does she do it, and how are her gifts received? Is there anything special about them?

_____

_____

_____

_____

_____

_____

_____

_____

_____

_____

_____

_____

_____

47. We have all heard stories about a wise old owl. Make up another wise creature, one that we would not expect to be wise. Tell a story that a child might enjoy. How about a wise hedgehog? Or a worm? Give them human names like Mary or Sue.

_____

_____

_____

_____

_____

_____

_____

_____

_____

_____

_____

_____

48. Write a story about a reclusive woman who only
writes stories on a typewriter and refuses to use
technology. Why?

_____

_____

_____

_____

_____

_____

_____

_____

_____

_____

_____

_____

49. Write a story of someone who is making a long journey and has to spend a night in an old English church. Write what happens. Why she is there?

_____

_____

_____

_____

_____

_____

_____

_____

_____

_____

_____

_____

_____

50. Think of a childhood memory that makes you feel shame or embarrassment. Write that story. Then rewrite it in a way that changes the ending.

_____

_____

_____

_____

_____

_____

_____

_____

_____

_____

_____

_____

51. Plan a list of random acts of kindness.

_____

_____

_____

_____

_____

_____

_____

_____

_____

_____

_____

_____

_____

_____

52. Make a list of places near where you live that you like to visit, write an article about your adventures and encourage people to visit (churches, lists of book swaps etc)

_____

_____

_____

_____

_____

_____

_____

_____

_____

_____

_____

_____

53. Write an acrostic poem. This is a poem which spells out a word vertically. Then write a line with the first letter of each word. Pick a word that you consider your favourite word and find creative words to explain why you like it so much. Basic example below:

Can't be bothered to come when called
Always hunting for mice
True friends
Sleeps the day away

_____

_____

_____

_____

_____

_____

_____

_____

_____

_____

_____

54. Write a conversation between two people while they are waiting for a cup of tea.

_____

_____

_____

_____

_____

_____

_____

_____

_____

_____

_____

_____

_____

55.Use one or more of these words and turn them into a positive: **http://www.stuff.co.nz/life-style/life/10459253/29-words-only-used-to-describe-women** in poetry/non-fiction, prose etc

airhead	ethereal beauty
ambitious	fawn-like
abrasive	headstrong
bossy	hormonal
bitchy	hysterical
bubbly	illogical
ditsy	motherly (2)
emotional	shrill
frigid	voluptuous
frumpy	whining
High Maintenance	working mum
pushy	
Sassy	
Bombshell	
Bitchy	
Breathless	
Bridezilla	
Curvy	

56. Write while listening to the birds outside, the silence and the sounds of nature.

_____

_____

_____

_____

_____

_____

_____

_____

_____

_____

_____

_____

_____

57. Find somewhere unusual to go and write, such as inside an old church.

_____

_____

_____

_____

_____

_____

_____

_____

_____

_____

_____

_____

_____

_____

58. Are you feeling writer's block? Ignore the voices that say you can't write. Grab a pencil or a computer and just free-write anything that comes to your head. Set a timer for 15 minutes and don't stop until the timer stops. Don't worry about what you say. Don't try to write a masterpiece. Just write everything that comes to your mind.

_____

_____

_____

_____

_____

_____

_____

_____

_____

_____

_____

_____

59. Turn on a favourite song. Play it all the way through in a very quiet room (if possible use headphones) and listen to the lyrics or music carefully. Analyse the song and try to imagine why the songwriter chose those words. Can you imagine what they were thinking or feeling when they wrote that song? If the song has no lyrics, what does the music say to you? What feelings does the music invoke?

_____

_____

_____

_____

_____

_____

_____

_____

_____

_____

_____

60. Go on a walk in nature and find a small object to take home to inspire you to write about it, or where you have been.

_____

_____

_____

_____

_____

_____

_____

_____

_____

_____

_____

_____

61. Choose a place you like to visit near where you live and write an article encouraging people to visit it too.

_____

_____

_____

_____

_____

_____

_____

_____

_____

_____

_____

_____

_____

_____

62. Write a phone conversation between two female characters. Imaginary ones, or borrowed characters from books/tv/film.

_____

_____

_____

_____

_____

_____

_____

_____

_____

_____

_____

_____

_____

63. Write a letter to your favourite author (even if they are dead).

_____

_____

_____

_____

_____

_____

_____

_____

_____

_____

_____

_____

_____

_____

_____

64. The story of a refugee girl in WW1 or 2 in a very big house in the middle of nowhere.

_____

_____

_____

_____

_____

_____

_____

_____

_____

_____

_____

_____

_____

_____

65. Go to Youtube and type in "Writer's Block Meditation" scroll until you find one that looks interesting, use headphones (if possible) and find a quiet, calm place to listen. Afterwards, free-write for 15 minutes about whether or not this helped your creativity.

_____

_____

_____

_____

_____

_____

_____

_____

_____

_____

_____

_____

66. Write a love letter to yourself.

_____

_____

_____

_____

_____

_____

_____

_____

_____

_____

_____

_____

_____

_____

67. Write about someone who works in a bookshop but has trouble keeping the characters in the books.

_____

_____

_____

_____

_____

_____

_____

_____

_____

_____

_____

_____

_____

68. Write about a child who, every time they walk through a doorway, they see a white drip fall from the ceiling to the floor. What is it and why is it happening?

_____

_____

_____

_____

_____

_____

_____

_____

_____

_____

_____

_____

_____

69. Write a ghost story with these ideas: A couple is driving home from a party. Perhaps one had too much to drink, they drive through a wooded area that they have always known and all of a sudden nothing looks familiar. It is dark and it begins to snow very heavily. They have an accident. Either hitting a tree, an animal or another car. Write about what happens after that.

_____

_____

_____

_____

_____

_____

_____

_____

_____

_____

_____

_____

70. Write a list of flowers that make you happy and decorate the page with pictures or drawings of them.

_____

_____

_____

_____

_____

_____

_____

_____

_____

_____

_____

_____

_____

_____

71. Create a female villain. What makes her tick? What makes her angry? What does she do when she is angry, sad, provoked? Sketch your character out by imagining every single detail about them from the way they look, foods they eat, books they like, places they have lived, what is their family like? Try to find a way to invoke empathy for the villain. Give them some likeable traits.

_____

_____

_____

_____

_____

_____

_____

_____

_____

_____

_____

_____

72. Write a story about an evil Elf-on-the-Shelf. Maybe they change facial expressions based on how the children behave. (If this is too scary for you, make a doll or toy come to life in magical, helpful way)

_____

_____

_____

_____

_____

_____

_____

_____

_____

_____

_____

_____

_____

73. Who are the fictional characters who have shaped you as a person and why?

_____

_____

_____

_____

_____

_____

_____

_____

_____

_____

_____

_____

_____

74. "When you read a book as a child, it becomes a part of your identity in a way that no other reading in your whole life does." - Meg Ryan as Kathleen Kelly in You've Got Mail.
What books were these for you?

_____

_____

_____

_____

_____

_____

_____

_____

_____

_____

_____

_____

75. Create an imaginary place. Close your eyes and imagine that you are sitting in the middle of a scene from your story. What does the ground or floor feel like? Are you inside or outside? What colour is the sky? Are there buildings around you? Trees? Flowers? Are you alone? What does it smell like? Is it summer or winter? Are you feeling anything? Take time to write every detail. Once you get all of the details, go back and use your words to write a descriptive scene for a story.

_____

_____

_____

_____

_____

_____

_____

_____

_____

_____

_____

76. Go for a walk and write down words that automatically come to mind from how you feel/what you see/hear etc, then come home, write those words on paper and cut them or rip them up to create an art journal page with the words and drawings or images.

_____

_____

_____

_____

_____

_____

_____

_____

_____

_____

_____

_____

77. Write a character study of one of your favourite characters, then use this to write one for a character of your own.

_____

_____

_____

_____

_____

_____

_____

_____

_____

_____

_____

_____

_____

78. Take a few of your favourite characters and explore why each one is one of your favourites, take parts of these characters to create your own original character and plot a story (of any length) around that character. Write that story.

_____

_____

_____

_____

_____

_____

_____

_____

_____

_____

_____

_____

79. Write a list of things you appreciate about someone
you love and give it to them.

_____

_____

_____

_____

_____

_____

_____

_____

_____

_____

_____

_____

_____

_____

80. Write down all of the words that you associate with grief. Take that list and arrange them into a poem of how it feels to grieve. This grief can be for a person, a pet, or even a way of life that you have lost.

_____

_____

_____

_____

_____

_____

_____

_____

_____

_____

_____

_____

_____

81. Try looking out of your window and writing a stream of consciousness piece about everything you see/hear.

_____

_____

_____

_____

_____

_____

_____

_____

_____

_____

_____

_____

_____

82. Take the first and last lines from one page in a book of your choice and re-write what happens in between as an original piece of poetry or fiction.

_____

_____

_____

_____

_____

_____

_____

_____

_____

_____

_____

_____

_____

83. Look at your bookshelf. Find the titles of 10-20 books. Write them all down and try to make a poem using all of your titles.

_____

_____

_____

_____

_____

_____

_____

_____

_____

_____

_____

_____

_____

_____

84. Write an article or essay about something unusual that you are very knowledgeable or interested in, like an object, place, person or time in history.

_____

_____

_____

_____

_____

_____

_____

_____

_____

_____

_____

_____

_____

_____

85. Imagine you are walking into a ~~museum~~ art gallery or. Every time you look at a piece of art, you are taken into the painting and become part of it. Which paintings would you want to see? Write about the worlds you get to explore.

British Museum. The House of stolen goods.

Sutton Hoo Ship Burial.

86. Write a flash fiction piece that is mostly dialogue.

87, Write a story inspired by one of the Bloomsbury Group.

_____

_____

_____

_____

_____

_____

_____

_____

_____

_____

_____

_____

_____

_____

88. Describe either a garden or a table full of food with as much intensely rich detail as possible, covering all of the senses, and an abundance of colour so that it would be impossible to cram any more description into it.

_____

_____

_____

_____

_____

_____

_____

_____

_____

_____

_____

_____

_____

89. Think about one of your all-time favourite characters in a TV series or book. Write a story about that character doing something that they would never normally do. Turn them into your own character.

_____

_____

_____

_____

_____

_____

_____

_____

_____

_____

_____

_____

_____

90. Write a piece of fan-fiction, take the characters you love from a television programme and practise writing in (and staying in) character by writing a scene or a story, or chapter of their lives. You can practise by copying the dialogue from a short scene to get a feel for the way the characters speak and interact (including the important noises of hesitation), then writing your own.

_____

_____

_____

_____

_____

_____

_____

_____

_____

_____

_____

_____

91. Write a story about a person who does not realize they are a ghost until they see that they leave no footprints in the snow, or some other thing that jolts them into realizing they are dead.

_____

_____

_____

_____

_____

_____

_____

_____

_____

_____

_____

_____

_____

92. Write a story about an animal that is a healing animal. This animal can feel their human's feelings as they happen. They are always there when you are crying, always happy when you are. Then write a scene in which they heal a person who is ill or depressed. What happens? Does this drain the animal of their power each time? Do they become more powerful every time they heal someone?

_____

_____

_____

_____

_____

_____

_____

_____

_____

_____

_____

_____

93. Write the story of a little girl who is unusual in a very unusual way, e.g. Matilda and her powers of telekinesis.

_____

_____

_____

_____

_____

_____

_____

_____

_____

_____

_____

_____

_____

_____

94. Write the stories of the inhabitants of a very small English village, when they all meet up in the middle of the village because something unusual has happened. What has happened? How do they interact with each other? How well do they know each other and who are they?

_____

_____

_____

_____

_____

_____

_____

_____

_____

_____

_____

_____

95. Write a story about a house that moves it's rooms around if it doesn't like a person who is visiting the owner of it. A house that doesn't behave if it feels it or it's owner, or the owners cat are threatened and seeks revenge on those who mistreat it.

_____

_____

_____

_____

_____

_____

_____

_____

_____

_____

_____

_____

96. Visit a book swap and find a book or magazine that you can use to create black out poetry in, or use to cut out words and create new writing from.

_____

_____

_____

_____

_____

_____

_____

_____

_____

_____

_____

_____

97. You have a very special dream catcher that gives you the power to dream whatever you want to dream at night. Write a poem or story about how your dreams will unfold.

_____

_____

_____

_____

_____

_____

_____

_____

_____

_____

_____

_____

_____

98. Imagine looking in the mirror when you first wake up and the face that you see is not yours. Why? What happened?

_____

_____

_____

_____

_____

_____

_____

_____

_____

_____

_____

_____

_____

_____

99. Write a poem with these 5 words in any order: glass, cat, moon, mansion, shenanigans

_____

_____

_____

_____

_____

_____

_____

_____

_____

_____

_____

_____

_____

_____

100. Your child discovers a fairy garden in the back garden. You smile and pat their head like an adult. Then you happen to see it while gardening. Write a short story about the fairies that live in your garden.

_____

_____

_____

_____

_____

_____

_____

_____

_____

_____

_____

_____

_____

101. Try to write funny. A diary entry written by a character from a book/tv show etc, or dialogue between two people that might make the reader or viewer laugh.

_____

_____

_____

_____

_____

_____

_____

_____

_____

_____

_____

_____

_____

Printed in Great Britain
by Amazon